SCARED
VIOLENT
LIKE
HORSES

poems

JOHN MCCARTHY

MILKWEED EDITIONS

Published 2019 by Milkweed Editions
Printed in Canada
Cover design by Mary Austin Speaker
Cover art by Joe Goode: *House Tornado (11521)*, 2007. Acrylic over lithograph.
Image by Alan Shaffer for Leslie Sacks Gallery.
Author photo by Andrew Hemmert
19 20 21 22 23 5 4 3 2 1
First Edition

Milkweed Editions, an independent nonprofit publisher, gratefully acknowledges sustaining support from the Jerome Foundation; the McKnight Foundation; the National Endowment for the Arts; the Target Foundation; and other generous contributions from foundations, corporations, and individuals. Also, this activity is made possible by the voters of Minnesota through a Minnesota State Arts Board Operating Support grant, thanks to a legislative appropriation from the arts and cultural heritage fund, and a grant from Wells Fargo. For a full listing of Milkweed Editions supporters, please visit milkweed.org.

Library of Congress Cataloging-in-Publication Data

Names: McCarthy, John (John Justin), 1990- author.
Title: Scared violent like horses : poems / John McCarthy.
Description: First edition. | Minneapolis, Minnesota : Milkweed Editions,
    2019. | Includes bibliographical references.
Identifiers: LCCN 2018031619 (print) | LCCN 2018032122 (ebook) | ISBN
    9781571319975 (ebook) | ISBN 9781571315076 (pbk. : alk. paper)
Classification: LCC PS3613.C345765 (ebook) | LCC PS3613.C345765 A6 2019
    (print) | DDC 811/.6--dc23
LC record available at https://lccn.loc.gov/2018031619

CONTENTS

III.

SCARED

VIOLENT

LIKE

HORSES

SWITCHGRASS

This is the year of this is never over. It's raining
and it will not stop raining. Outside Springfield,
roads move like spilled water. Silos of dirt and rust
surround the bones of barn lofts with shingles shucked
like broken stalks. Crabapple trees lose their fruit
and fall from rot into wild clover. In the straight lines
of cut lawns—the hay-thick scent of Illinois.
Plowed hillsides pierced by stenciled signs beg me
to pray to God. The switchgrass bends to the shoulder
of the road, pushing the wind through the gravel.
The switchgrass sways and sways. It will not stop swaying.
I'm floating away from home. I'm becoming a prayer
I never said for myself. There is smolder and silence
when my pickup truck goes quiet and smoke rises
from the engine. Parked slanted on the road's shoulder,
it takes a few tries with wet fingers to prop the hood.
A mangled cat mats the crankshaft and fan belt,
fur-shredded and soaked. He must have wanted
warmth from the storm when my truck was a box
of rust resting crooked on my lawn, miles ago.
His black eyes are rolled back. His tongue is out
and his throat is ripped open, exposing muscle.
I never even heard his scream, piston-stretched
and hot. I want to shake him back to life,
but I feel so far away. It's raining and it will not stop
raining. Switchgrass quivers in every direction.
It's raining, and I don't have anywhere to leave.

I

HYMN

The low song a lost boy sings remembering his mother's call.
—BRIGIT PEGEEN KELLY

I was a lost boy with a quiet ache, so quiet it was like listening
to a spider weave a web around a cotton ball in early autumn.

The temperature dropped. The trees breathed *please* with their long breaths.
My throat grew raw and thick in the scratched-open light of morning

when I woke nervous and cold. I found my naked feet bare
and the bed covers fallen from the bed with the fan left on.

My mother was still gone like good sleep. I've never had a conversation
with my mother about our lost days or anything other than how I'm cold.

She can't have a conversation because her geography is mapped
with a landscape of broken light bulbs and brown leaves and dirty snow

that is so dirty it looks like the variegated feathers of a lost boy
with lost wings. And that boy remembers his mother singing *hallelujah*

in church, and I remember being at church the whole time wanting
to be in the trees, hiding and feeling the trees breathing *please*

against my cold skin—*please*. All the while, my father sits
in a checkered lawn chair, even when it's cold outside, with a small radio

listening to baseball scores recount the losses of men who have lost
their whole lives swinging at a ball. That ball is sometimes a bird

that a boy reaches for as the bird edges the sky. My father rubs his hands
on his knees and yells, and I'm yelling in the trees about missing everything

that I have lost—a song I once heard at church that goes *Lady, help the absent loved ones. How we miss their presence here. May the hand of thy protection guide*

and guard them far and near. I don't know how it goes anymore. The air is plain like the color of my forearm, and I'm sitting in a children's swimming pool

that has deflated to a swarming puddle of mosquitoes. It is scum-thick, and I'm trying to sing *help the absent,* but I'm a lost boy who can't remember

that lost song, that can't remember how to sing his *hallelujah,* so I sit scratching the red bites on my legs until they bleed.

PIE TINS BEHIND PORCH LIGHTS

August and it's battery-hot again like the sun has been turned on for days.
  Mother is sweating; and she has stuffed pie tins behind our porch lights

to keep the robins from nesting. The spangled rays of sun reflecting
  off the tins illuminate her grief, her illness—shards of light

above her head like a broken halo. A moat of silence stretches
  around our house. Her voice is missing in the wind, and the stalks

in the field run into each other in their panic, and their whispers
  crawl out and knock on our door like a newspaper thrown sidelong

by a kid on a bike. My mother crosses that threshold each day like wading
  into deep water, vanishing from the feet up. She answers the door

until there is nothing. All year I remember it has been like this—
  bags of makeup, unused, spilled across the bathroom floor,

her clothes, too baggy for her body, fastened to her ankles and wrists
  with rubber bands as she moves through the house

like a dial tone. The phone doesn't ring anymore but mother answers
  anyway, listening for the voices passing through her body

PORTRAIT OF THE ONLY CHILD WITH TIRE SWING

The cornfield's tassels are wicks burning toward the sky, and the fields
are sutured by utility poles marching like a procession of crosses.

On one side of the field I-55 stretches out, and semitrucks vibrate
with that low drone of travelling forever, flashing their lights at one another—
Hello, I'm here, Goodbye—and they continue on alone. On the other side

of the field the only child hums a song of loneliness and mourning
but he doesn't know that yet. He thinks only of how the song sounds

nice and matches the corn's swaying as he sits on the edge
of his tire swing, gripping the twisted triangle of rusted chain that twirls
and pinches his fingers, his legs dangling through the center of the tire.

The only child imagines this center to be the mouth of a very large slide
or a cave whose darkness is the entrance to some foreign and exotic place

where flowers without names unfurl towards him like handshakes.
But he is afraid to enter such dark tunnels alone. Everything is unknown,
and his humming grows louder as he spins faster and mistakes his dizziness

for permanence, and there is no one around him to tell him how still
and quiet the fields of Illinois really are. The semi-trucks speed through,

and their echoing whirs can be counted on like heartbeats.
When the only child falls off the swing and everything above him spins,
he believes every organ inside his body is a heart. All he does is throb.

SELF-PORTRAIT AS STOLEN BIKE

I'm moving under a force I don't know. One minute, I'm two years old and on my side in a front yard surrounded by sunflowers and lawn ornaments. The next minute some big hands are gripping me tighter than I've ever been gripped before. Someone who I don't know and can't see is controlling me. Before now, I've only known the power of *goddamn* from the mouth of a small boy, so this must be a new *goddamn* because I'm going faster than I've ever gone. I'm in a new home now, a new garage. The light fades from a different angle and faster when the door shuts. Everything around here slams shut with more force. Everything seems more final. I was once the only bike in the garage. There are twenty others now. Some are cleaner. Some are sadder. Some have pedals scraped at the plastic edges like a scoop of ice cream that has been licked and is starting to melt. When you're alone long enough in the dark it's hard to hold onto the last memory you want to keep: that first day I emerged from my old garage, where a boy edged me past a tan Oldsmobile and rode me to St. Aloysius elementary. I waited all day between the rust slats of a bike rack with a chain threaded through my spokes like a stationed horse. The bikes around me were clean and new and proud. Where are those friends now? I remember the sound of a bell. I remember how excited all of those children seemed when they came running back to us at the end of the day.

Softening into dark gray, the silver layer of evening folds over
the old two-quarter carousel horse I'm riding outside the IGA corner store.
My grandmother is inside
buying lottery tickets with her savings.

I'm gripping the white handles
bolted to the horse's brayed face. Kicked open, the sculpting of the stomach
is caverned, the edges of its pink cast metal frame fractured white.

I wonder if I'm small enough to curl up inside, vanish.
I'm swaying
on the horse, and I wish my mother were here, taking my picture
with a disposable camera,
but I'm the yellow humming
of a corner store doorway. I dismount the horse,
and the empty parking lot watches.

Dark garbage stuffs the horse's stomach—
cigarette wrappers, plastic pop bottles, wet receipts,
and I scrape out its empty body. It feels like biting the tongs of a fork
when my nails scrape its metal cast.
There are dead insects, too, and I feel like dead insects.

I stick my head into the hollow of its stomach. That's all that fits.
In the dark,
I hear my grandmother call me *A gross thing*. *Get out*, she says.

She won twenty dollars from a scratch-off
but only has five left to show. When she hands me two loose quarters
from the bottom of her bingo bag,
I climb up the horse's mechanical canter.

She lights a cigarette and waves smoke away like swatting flies,

                              and I think of the horse's caverned body,
how comfortable it would be to live inside.

My grandmother lights her cigarettes on the toaster's orange electric coils,
then slaps at the smoke like she is batting at a man or a ghost or a curtain

nicotine-stained from exhaling all of her old years filled with smoke.
When she parts that curtain, she watches me drape my grandfather's clothes

over the chain-link fence to dry in the August sun. I made the mistake of saying,
I'm bored, so now I'm useful.

My grandfather is driving his truck over a gravel path,

and it sounds like an arm twisting around inside a bucket of acorns.
He is on his far-off way into the windy field to pick apples and grapes.

I want to know what it's like out there in the acorn and apple trees, tangled
in the grape vines as the light falls through the leaves onto my body. I imagine

my grandfather plucking and pinching a piece of fruit between his dirty fingernails,
muttering some old song of labor. When he tests his work with a bite and feels

the juice running down his chin, it will make me think of the blood
that ran down mine when he plucked a tooth from my mouth—

the way an apple sometimes needs to be turned and violently snapped
from its wet branch. My grandfather attacked most things like this.

Once the tooth was out, he slapped me on the ass and sent me outside
to bleed for an hour, nicked up and shivering like deer legs.

Now I'm trembling again,

beating out my grandfather's shirt, pit-stained with circles of olive-colored sweat
smelling of apples and grapes. I look up and wave at my grandmother,

her face is a cloud of yellow curtain and curling smoke, and the squint in her eye
acknowledges the fear of the wet shirt I'm holding as if the shirt were standing up

straight, hand raised like it was full of the body belonging to the man in the field.

HUNGER

This is how my mother leaves me—the clean points of a fork
pressing into my tongue. She stands over the stove, adrift
in the boiling water, steam blurring her face. It's been weeks now,
and the medication releases cotton into her bloodstream,
swelling her tongue and wrists. Like cleaning out a shower drain,
my mother pulls loose hair from her scalp, nail-picked and dry.
Her hands are side effects, twitching, and in the ditch
behind our house, my father burns leaves in a trash barrel.
Smoke billows through our open window like a freezer
pulled open in a warm room.
                                While my legs dangle
from the chair, I imagine the flowers on the wallpaper
wilting off, filling my empty bowl like cicada shells
or wood shavings. After straining the macaroni, my mother
scrapes it into the trash. She says *These things will kill us.*
She has begun talking like this again about food. My father
comes inside. My mother changes her story. Her explanation—
He's too old to eat something so silly. My father doesn't believe her
and goes back outside. My mother floats to her bedroom
where she sinks into bed like a dish to the bottom of the sink.

WORD PROBLEM

Imagine you want to make three Mother's Day cards. It will take you seventeen minutes
to make the cards. If you began at 8:00am, what time will you finish the three cards?
—FOUND ON AN ELEMENTARY SCHOOL MATH WORKSHEET

Let's say I didn't want to make the cards. Let's say it took years to never finish.
Let's say I started but each minute fell away and caved down to the tiny finch bones

time is made of. Let's say my relationship with my mother was complicated
by the fact she kept trying to die every day regardless of the time. She wanted to die.

I almost gave my mother a box of rocks one year, but didn't. I got scared and ran away
into a field and threw the rocks at an old brown barn. There were cows in the field

next to the barn. I remember my father once called my mother a cow
so I threw rocks at the cow heads. They mooed and sounded like music. I laughed,

but I knew this was sad. The same day I got dropped into this world of wondering
about my mother and time, I grew very bored and angry. I kept throwing

rocks at cows and barns until a barn owl erupted from the haymow screeching
like a tire burning out. The barn owl flew into my mouth and nested in my throat.

Every day afterward at 8:00am when I woke, opened the fridge to grab a glass of milk
and yawned, my mother saw the barn owl staring at her from the back of my throat.

Let's say the barn owl explained why, instead of *I love you*, my mother said, *That's strange*,
or *Why would you do that?* I asked her the same things. Let's say after failing

to write even one card, I went to my teacher explaining my failure as a son,
and my teacher said, *Keep on trying*. In a moment of anger, I said the same thing

to my mother later that day. My mother should have broke down in tears, but didn't.
Her face stayed the same, and I couldn't help but think I said the wrong thing

because my mother gave the wrong answer, so I ran outside and kept running
past all the fields and barns until I was far enough away to send a card, but didn't.

CREMATION

My father burned our dog,
and I never got my hands dirty
with ash resin or felt the air
of a sad wind after goodbye.
He told me he left her
in a white room with a hot oven
and walked away. It was too hard
to do anything else. I had
just got home from school
when I began to think of her
burning alone like the squirrel
my friends trapped. They pinned
its neck in the teepee frame
of the cord wood and sparked a fire.
In my backyard, when the fire
dwindled to smolder, the squirrel's
head was alive, screaming
a goddamned sound beyond
screaming. No fur left on its face.
No eyelids. We felt a terror
of doing wrong, of watching
a thing so dead still twitch
trying to hang on. I ran
to the shed, grabbed a hammer.
I came out hollering, hitting
the skull so hard it stopped.
I had to I had to, I told my friends.
They had no eyelids watching me
smash the body of a suffering thing.
My dog was still alive then,
chewing on a stick and leashed

to a stake in the yard. I did
not think about her at all
as I kneeled back down
and got the fire going again.

NOISE FALLING BACKWARD

I've been told not to come here—to this toolshed of memory,
where everything is as old as it is useless. Inside, a scoop of millet seed

      balances on a mulch sack. There are garbage bags full
of crushed Natural Light cans exhaling. Trespassing, I feel

like everything is a discovery—the open slat window, the salt licks

meant for nesting in the laps of tree stumps, the way the dust meanders
through the light like a premonition.

           Outside, mare's tail clouds run wild and smear the sky orange
at the end of a long day, and a hummingbird feeder hangs from the mulberry.
      No one has come for me yet. Silence is just noise falling backward

      from the future, and I don't know what to do with it.
I haven't lived through it yet. It's like wiping my eyes in the rain.

      I can't see clearly. I can't get a grip on anything. Alone here,
I linger and thumb the empty hull of a shotgun shell. There are more

long days ahead. For now, everything is quiet and mutable.
      I wish the present could stay like this—in its place and hidden.

NORTH END II

Plastic IGA bags like crumpled pieces of paper
       surround the feet of a man begging for change on a pigeon-stained walkway.

        He reincarnates each morning
in front of the grocer with his styrofoam cup and its rattling galaxies
      of loose change. *Don't give him a quarter,* my mother says
         as she paces ahead of me.

She thinks his situation means he can't hear her,
      and I'm not old enough to know how to apologize to him,

      or realize that my mother's fear is the same as his. That everything
is a cardboard scene that could be ripped away at any nauseating moment,

        but only if one of us has the privilege to do so.

Instead we pretend to forget each other and in turn we are forgotten
together, as a whole. And our side of town makes no noise

      except for the empty bottles thrown from car windows
at night, ushered by the faint murmuring of televisions turned up too loud.

        In this moment of listening to my mother
pretend that this man does not exist—the last few teeth in his mouth
      enormous in their loneliness, his winter coat
         spilling its down feathers in the August heat—

I learn how we deny each other, daily, so many chances to care.

CALLOUSING

November grew strong with the year's last roughshod fury
of the Johnson farm boys who soaked their fists in petrol oil
to harden their hits. They desired one last fight before December

cloaked them in Carhartts, made them split logs in snow glinting
with blue sparks of sunlight like a stadium filled with cameras
going off, which lets them imagine a sense of accomplishment

they will never feel. This was why they went driving around
in lettermans, hats bill-bent with fishhooks, hunting for someone
to judge with their broad shoulders. I hid from them

as long as I could on those lengthened nights when I walked
home alone. No one was with me in that darkness. The Johnsons
were strong and lacked nothing. I was weak. It was the fall,

and it was time for the Johnsons to pretend they were God.
They cut me off in their truck, striking me down and slapping
my mouth open. They made me say their names. The Johnsons

held me on the ground while I cradled my head and guarded
my face with bent elbows, but their violence was smart enough
to stop before I got too hurt. They piled back into their truck,

leaving me with wind-gone lungs, the humiliation of their spit
on my body, and my wide, corrupted smile that couldn't stop
grinning through a swollen lip and a knotted forehead, panting

like a dog struck sideways and dumb by some hand from above.
Praise this—this memory I rise with all the days of my life. Praise
this—that which breaks only to harden.

SELF-PORTRAIT AS HOME RUN BALL

For now this is the only thing—this fence and over it the barbed thistle and thin briar where I have dropped out of the air. The boys playing start arguing if I am a homerun or an automatic out because someone will have to hop the fence, reach in, and feel around for my red stitching, which feels like two centipedes crawling away from each other. When they decide I am the tying run, the boy who hit me rounds the bases. His team hollers at him, and the sun begins to set. But I belong to the boy climbing the cyclone fence to fetch me. He is the only boy wearing long sleeves, and those sleeves are attached to the only nice shirt he has, which is supposed to be worn to church tomorrow. When he lifts me out of the bushes and holds me up with his thorn-snagged sleeve, his team yells, *Hurry up*. But I see the look on his face, the lawn sprinklers waving back and forth like paper fans, the cicadas and their dim crescendoing dirge, and the panicgrass that the boy runs back through as he realizes what fetching me will cost him. His face looks like a boy who fears the wrath of God. He thinks how God is like a father who will twist the top of his ear down toward his cheek, leading him across a knee. He thinks of all the blood that will rush to his cheeks and his jaw as he tries to explain sacrifice and the tears in his sleeves. The boy's father will take me away and place me on a high shelf as the boy tries to explain how it all had to go on.

THE SCARECROW'S REFLECTION IS AN ONLY CHILD

After it rains, the scarecrow looks down into the mud-rutted puddles
filled with water and admires his reflection. Sometimes he pretends

that his reflection is his brother or that all the puddles together
are a group of siblings that understand his strange body. The weight
of rain sloughs the straw jutting from his sleeves and collects at the base

of his support beam like a pile of needles. He strains to reach down
and put the straw back into his burlap body, but he is crucified

and forced to accept the weather of all four seasons forever.
The scarecrow wants to build another version of himself out of straw,
reflection, and desire. The scarecrow calls this hunger. In the dead

of summer, the scarecrow begs the sky to darken and make it rain
again so the puddles can fill. The scarecrow only wants to pretend

that he has a family. In this way, the rain feeds the scarecrow
only to make him hunger again. Everything leaves the scarecrow—
the cars passing through on the interstate, the crows pausing briefly

on electrical wires, splaying their wings only to offer caws then silence
after they alight. When the soybeans begin to grow, their fledgling

sprouts cover the puddles in the furrows. No longer can the scarecrow
look down and know himself or pretend that there is anyone
in his life to share the feeling of the strong wind against his body.

BLOODMEAL

My father squeezes his fork like a tired man growing into the patience
that waits for him at the end of a long day and that has gone on for years
in the direction of sorrow.

        I've just asked my mother, *Do you want to die,*
and my mother presses her knife into her throat—it is speculative,
the way the knife threatens to puncture, tensing taught her skin
with urge and dare.

        Not in front of the kid, my father says,
and I'm trying to listen for the swishing of the cicadas
coming through the screen door like the sawing rattle of the refrigerator,
but my mother has a silence for every occasion,

        even at dinner with the microwaved lasagna
slapped down on paper plates like a sack of bloodmeal, like a substance
some starving animal might look at bewildered before taking its chances.
I look my mother in the eyes,

        and she is staring through a window
at a tree that is not there. The tree was chopped and craned down
from our yard years ago, and I can feel the vinyl tablecloth
scratching my legs like gooseflesh,

        raising the hairs on my skin, the same way
the truth makes me weak and cold because it lets me know
my body can be pierced by her silence. I flinch, and I'm afraid
my mother's silence means *Yes, oh yes, but not yet.*

LITTLE TICKS OF BLOOD AND THE TASTE OF DEAD LEAVES

If we knew anything that day, it was my blood on a stem of burning wheat that we had lit and tried to smoke. We thought this was cool. The hair on our legs had started to darken and thicken like twitchgrass. We were bored, and boredom leads boys to make a dangerous novelty of what is otherwise common and beautiful—soft wheat patches bristling in the shade of lush trees. When a sweetgum ball fell from the branch above us, Seth dared me to bite down on it, and I couldn't stop spitting. Little ticks of blood and the taste of dead leaves shrank the world to that individual moment of shock. All of my spitting sounded like *you, you, you,* and Seth said, *I can't believe you actually did that.* He was leaning back and laughing with his arms folded across his chest like someone coming back from the dead. All of this was a trick. It was hot—so goddamn hot—and it hurt to chew a sweetgum ball. But I didn't mind. It felt good to have a friend who spent all day with me in the heat, trying to smoke a humid stem of wheat, a friend who laughed at all the things I did.

UNTIL I LEARN THAT *PLEASE* IS THE COLOR OF A BRUISE

Made from his hands, Chris aims a gun at me.
You're dead, he says. But I don't like being
the dead one, so I take off running. The chasing
lasts a long time. We snag our sleeves
on the tops of chain-link cyclone fences
until the chasing becomes a way to see
how far we can explore. Climb and run,
climb and run, the unbraiding of back alleys
and empty lots until we end up on an acreage
of private property with our own privacy
and no one else around. Chris corners me
under an old lean-to where a sun-damaged
cigarette boat is living out the rest of its existence
on top of an old hitch-trailer. Here,
Chris forces me to play punch-for-punch
until I beg *Please stop*. Until I learn that *please*
is the color of a bruise, skin swollen and purple
on the side of my throbbing arm. Everything is
swollen when it starts raining. We roll our pant legs
up and walk home through the wet grass.
My soaked shoes, as I walk, are like a feeling
knotting up inside my stomach that I can't explain.
This is how you stay friends when you're poor,
Chris says. Our whole summer was like this—
when we couldn't see that far into the future,
every day was the same. It was nice,
the way we could handle a little bit of pain
and return to it again, day after day.

NORTH END III

That was the year a red-and-yellow Fisher-Price car appeared on our porch,
       its body dented and scratched, its dirty roof covered in faded stickers
worn down to white adhesive.
              That was the year we had buckets in the kitchen
to catch water falling from a ceiling that thought it was the sky.

I sat on our porch in my car without windows
       and listened to the rain clink the plastic roof like a clicking stove burner.

That was the year I was always on fire because my shoes pinched my toes
       and my clothes never fit. That was the year our mailbox settled,
leaned to its side exhausted, its orange flag snapped off and its rusted front flap
       hung open like a fish's curved mouth.

         That was the year I was sent home from school for head lice,
for peeing my pants, for not changing my clothes, for never washing my hands.

I scratched my scalp with a cheese grater on the porch and cried all year.

         That was the year I wondered what year mom would come back.
That was the year her body came back like a plastic toy someone had shaken.
           That was the year she slept all year.

I carved my scalp open until I could feel the smoke leaving my body.

         That was the year I stepped on a nail
and my father slapped me around for the price of a tetanus shot.

         That was the year the neighboring houses woke up covered
in brown boards and spray paint shouting *Gas Off*. That was the year our neighbor

lost his job and got arrested for shooting squirrels with a shotgun in his yard
while I watched from a red-and-yellow car without moving.

That was the year that was longer than a year in Springfield—
gunshots—my father never speaking except to say *enough*.

VANDALISM

Rust and fumes form a dirge, a dune of umber in the falling sky,
 falling every night like a drape across the broomgrass and wild straw.
Henbit sprouts from the brown rock and root-split concrete.
 Scraps of leather and cloth hang frayed on the high fences,
wire-cut and pulled apart by thieves coming at night for copper scrap
 inside the Pillsbury Plant and its hollow guts. It is abandoned
and we are the abandoned sons of fathers who look for work while talking
 with their hands. *Do you think we'd work here,* I ask Seth, *if it didn't close?*
We walk on the train tracks cutting through the iron-laid yard
 where spare train cars halt and tilt on diverging turnouts waiting
for pick up by rail companies. This is the North End and it never changes.
 I raise my spray can and ask what I should tag on the rusted railcar.
We're both at a loss for words, already aware profanity doesn't get anyone
 to notice us. I push the nozzle down. I write my name instead.

FLYOVER COUNTRY

I. [If You Stay Long Enough]

Here is my only life—a hymn pushed into my tongue like weld screws—
       the pulsing of a cricket inside a crow's mouth.

For me, this flat land has held so much weight I'll collect its fragments—
       the gospels of vacant parking lots, the quietude of single lane

dirt roads. Off to the side, a new family watches their firstborn play
       in a sandbox at the edge of a cornfield where possums go

to die alone in the husks while we go on existing. Dying alone is a privilege
       of privacy, and here you can possess it without any artifice—

no tall churches or taller skyscrapers—here you can exit like waking
       to the chilled spring where ice sloughs off the evergreens,

and the shimmering reminds me of church bells, and the acorns
       unearth themselves amid the same dead-colored leaves

that go on living a buried life, keeping the garden bed warm. No place
       is sad if you stay long enough, and if you stay long enough,

come visit the last used bookstore that holds the yellowed almanacs
       and historical indexes on pallid steel shelves layered with dust,

the loud dreams of farmers whose voices can still be heard, even seen,
       their clothes billowing like flags strapped to a clothesline,

taut and bouncing over a steep sea of buffalograss. How else do I give
       names to the wraiths of a landscape? Here, harsh versions

of man's machinery tread through every year and, between each season,
      a space opens up and the sun unlocks a door in the ground

with its brightness, and if you imagine your ears to be a system of roots,
      let them burrow into soil and you will hear beyond this voice.

You will hear what solitude sounded like before it was alone—
      a speck of dirt, its body, hollering fervent and raw.

II. [Of Motherhood, a Fierce Drowning]

The incessant silence of the central Midwest drove my mother mad.

Between the gaps of noise, the undulating wind passed like public trains

between the rows of terraced houses in crowded cities. There was no peace

for her. She has never seen this world from any different angle, having lived

only in her parents' house and the house next door for fifty years.

To not move like that means to measure dust by the buckets of light

casting shadows on the wall each day until an invisible voice seizes

the skull and a landscape of zoysia invades the soft ground—infertile seeds

of motherhood and identity. When a life grows this small, turns this rough,

everything attacks it—the skinny arms of the gingko in our backyard,

the deformed fingers of the sweetgum dropping its dangers around the house

like traps. They were only trees swaying in the pale light of a blank bedroom wall

but it was like a wave that threatened to drag her under, and did, eventually—

a gentle rocking, then a violent thrashing, her depression a fierce drowning

between the slab lots of two houses that have settled forever at the bottom

of Springfield, Illinois. Sometimes, when her eyes stay open and she can't sleep, she will ask, *Do you hear the windchimes?* She hung them when she was nine

at her parent's house next door. *They're still ringing,* and I can hear them, too.

How comforting that must be to her, I think, then how terrifying.

III. [Long Day of the Factory Belt]

And what of my father who lost his father at nine?
            Everyday after he threw a baseball at a church wall
      across the street from the only apartment he ever knew,
               playing basketball on the sloped hill of a parking lot

with other lost kids on the North End, until he moved in
          with my mother in the only place she ever knew,
      and together, the two of them compared the only geographies
             they believed in.

When he thinks of this, his face reminds me of a barn's haymow
          rotting away, insulated with owl nests
     and mouse skulls. This was his descent
             into the incinerating pleasure of normalcy—

work and bars, work and bars—long days of the factory belt hangover.
          How many days has he risen and questioned
     the different versions of himself pinned to clotheslines
             where the wind flattened, smoothed, and beat

out the wrinkles? I believe it was hard for him to reach into a closet
          too small to contain the dreams that went missing
     and pull out a routinely painful, uniformed version
             of himself, like removing an arm from a bush,

finding it scratched by thistle and covered in cockleburs he pretends
          don't hurt. When I look into the landscape behind his eyes,
     I believe it was too much for him to sludge everyday
             through the sedgegrass shadowed

with sycamores and elms, where littered white plastic bags
           floated through like ghosts,
                 snagging on felled branches—yes, his eyes grew to look like this.
                       It took me a long time to accept this,

but his wife is asleep in a bed that is falling into the ground,
             and I will never understand his fear. Compassion
        is awareness of the ineffability of another's fear—its different shades,
                 and there is honor in the weathered crumpling of his face.

IV. [The Taste of Copper]

When I had a loose tooth, my father yanked it out with a wet rag.

Bloody at its root, he set the tooth on the counter,
said, *Keep it as a souvenir.*

He left me alone after,
        went to visit my mother in the hospital,

and I ran outside to plant my tooth
among the rotting A and R train tracks
behind our house, dismantled and stacked.

White clover blossoms were growing all around the scrap
        burning with the kind of rust that stained my hands orange.

I believed if I planted my teeth they would grow into white clover.

I shivered
as the wind entered through my sleeves.

I was barefoot, and dirt caked my heels.

The taste of copper was drying in my gum's black socket,
as if I had just licked a battery.

It was cold
and the white clover blossoms chattered
and flinched.

I lay down in the grass on my back.

I thought I would turn invisible—
the fleshy ends of white clover chewing the edges of my skin,
swallowing me into the dirt—

face up,

while the sky tried to remember the ground below.

V. [To Sever Anything]

It is always winter again and the gutted deer hang
        from their hoists and gambrels and lose their blood in the snow.

Sometimes the blood is in my hair. Sometimes my hair is on fire,
        and I'm singing to you with dirt in my mouth. I have no winter boots,

and my tennis shoes are wet with slush. The snow
        sounds like a jaw grinding its teeth in a very quiet room

as I walk away with a knife in my hand to try and sever
        all that makes me my father and my mother and these states

crooked and flat with nothing in them and no one important,
        until I decide that's not true. I don't want to sever anything.

I have to walk back to the deer hooked and hanging
        with its legs spread like a drunk man leaning out of a car window

with his arms splayed and his eyes rolling back into his head
        as he tries to see the sky one last time before the black out.

This deer. This beautiful animal I'm slicing and dressing—
        its liver and intestines fill my hands. My nails are so deep in blood

they look caked with dirt. It's so cold, and I can't stop wiping snot
        from under my nose. My skull tries to suck it all back up.

It sounds like a throttle choking. I stab the skinning knife into the thigh,
        tear the pelt away from the muscle—this, the only life I know.

VI. [To Riven Stillness]

The first time I heard my friend say *flyover country* I had no clue I should have taken offense, but I was young and rising five days a week to work at a parking garage with relapsing alcoholics and sex offenders who tried to offer me advice in the form of cocaine knotted tightly in the cellophane from a cigarette box. I wanted to stay there forever because I wanted what was familiar and what was comfortable to remain the same. I was dumb, too, and I thought every place was the same then, whether in Iowa or Indiana, Missouri or Ohio. All their drugs were the same—a vacant parking lot and a shaking of hands. All the breadlines were the same, too, smelling of antiseptic with twelve inch TVs holding auxiliary cables in with scotch tape, the linoleum tile gone gray under a thin layer of dust and scuff, black streaks from the chairs scooting, and canned food stacked like tin pillars piled next to cracker boxes inside laundry baskets. And it was at a breadline somewhere outside of St. Louis—its frowning arch far off in the distance of clouds—that I let a man sell me baking soda in a Ziploc bag because he needed the money for a life out of his control. My friend and I wanted a free meal before driving across state lines with a pound of marijuana under my old baby blankets in the back of a station wagon. We got a deal on the pot and wanted to sell it and keep driving. We both talked like we had a little too much hope. I made a phone call and quit my job, and we drove on. That night, the moon was as thin and yellow as a toenail clipping. Everything was quiet and free, and it taught me how to riven stillness out of any given place. No two spaces are alike, and it made sense when we pulled off at a rest stop. We sat on a bench, staring up at a passing plane. The lights on its wings flashed. The plane pulled the clouds over the moon like a stage curtain. *They're just looking down, right here, calling us flyover country.* He said it soft. He seemed like a person who had just been profoundly affected by the sudden return of an unfamiliar memory—

VII. [Renders and Yields]

When the speck of dirt sings from its fallow field abandoned
   by harvest and covered with frost, a boredom emerges in that cold time,

and patience is tried. It's like watching an icicle melt, drop by drop,
   from a gutter only to freeze again on the old porch

black from the fall's unswept leaf rot. I have spent lifetimes inside
   watching a house being dismantled and rebuilt out of sunlight

and freezing temperatures, but this is how I learned patience,
   how to control my burning, the way switchgrass looks

like a scalp of hair on fire nodding back and forth in the wind.
   When the thaw begets spring and a vastness unveils a roadside ditch,

a green rectangular population sign counts the number of people
   within its small city limits, in Illinois, where farmers thresh the wheat,

and the windmills go on pushing the clouds away from the sky
   to let the light down on the water towers that look like giant golf tees

poised and waiting for any benevolent hand to swing the weather,
   scything their tops across green waves. When the dirt sings,

a field of birds scatter in an unrecognizable pattern, and mystery is tilled
   as the sky widens out from the ground and vanishes everywhere.

Such soft violence renders and yields this truth—each place is different
   in its silence, in its upward reaching fields. It dares you

to misunderstand its rhythm, its landlocked and landmarked song—
   the imperfect order of the prairie's flailing, wild flutter.

III

SCARED VIOLENT LIKE HORSES

I was too young to call him a friend, but I had a classmate once who snuck up
               behind a horse and now his body is made of a long time ago.
    He is the quiet space in my memory where he never sat next to me again.
                    Back then, everyone I ever called a friend held fire in their fists
when they talked to me. Their fists were dingy, grime-covered, and grease-slick
           as if they were made of horsehair, as if they were untamed and lonely,
       galloping and wind-swollen. We didn't know how to talk about loss,
              so we made each other lose. We went to fields to see
who could take the most damage. We went to fields that smelled like the boy
          who became an empty space on a Tuesday morning a long time ago.
    Now, because I am scared of time and how it moves, I look down at my fists
              that didn't always want to, but have hit so many friends
that the broken knuckles look like bruised magnolias. Listen to me, *Please*,
         when I knock or bang on the table or door and beg for attention.
    Please, I don't know how to ask for forgiveness. I don't know how
             to let anything go. I don't know how to say anything else
about the boy who had a buzz cut and a flat head, the boy who was kicked in the face
         by a horse and died looking up at the sky. The boy's father must have
       found his son with a crushed face, and while running back to the house
           with his own son in his arms, must have said something raging
and spiteful to God. This memory is my starting point when I think backward
          and apologize for all of our fists coiled tight as key rings. How could we not
break the mirror we look at in the morning? How could we not swing
         at the different versions of our faces staring back between
the fissures? The hurt and mangled parts of us loved the blood dried brown
         on our skewbald knuckles, and we had nightmares of being reined in.
   We needed someone to help us change. We needed someone to force us
         into confronting the uselessness of our violence.
But no one came, and our fists swelled unbridled and restless, wild and afraid.

THE DECAPITATION OF PAUL BUNYAN

After the 2006 tornado in Sangamon County

The sky is still gnarled-iron gray from the tornado that hit
four days ago. Shade trees leak rain. The Best Buy sign
is shaped like Pennsylvania in its blown out black-wire frame.
Potholes fill with water grizzled silver like detached hubcaps.
Mini-vans, dented as the Diet Coke can my father crushes,
glint in the parking lot, and I am driving my father
to buy new shoes on the west side after bailing him out
from the drunk tank. I want to be anywhere but Illinois
next to this bald man sucking his fingernails,
worried about the holes in his heels. We don't know
each other. Father and son—call us shadows. Call us
storm-split trees. Call us every split husk folded open
to the light breaking through. When I check the turn lane
our eyes lock like we're strangers waiting in a long line.
At a red light, a twenty-foot statue of Paul Bunyan
towers headless, advertising Lauterbach Tires
like an ancient wonder of a once great city. One palm turns
upward, the other holds a nickel of sky where an ax handle
used to be. The statue's red flannel collar is like a grin
with no face. When the light changes, I drive on.
My father's presence is a fitful, inconstant wind.
He says, *Turn here.* Gutters fill with wet sticks, and I know
he feels empty-handed, like there's no head on his shoulders.

THIN NAPKINS SPRINKLED WITH SALT

I followed my father's lead like finding footprints in the snow
as he walked into *Newtz* with its dart-holed cork held together
with duct tape, its bar stools specked with the neon shine
of old slot machines and glitch-tune sounds of video poker.
Newtz, my father said, meant *North End White Trash*.

I imagined the space his body took up while leaning into his friends
telling his sad stories, letting his friends share their sad stories
until they all had enough sadness to stop. Sadness is made of thin napkins
sprinkled with salt. For years, people called our family *Newtz*, listened
as my friends bragged that they were *Newtz*. And on this night,

I was starting one of those nights that belonged to a long line of years
when Sam, a former classmate, walked in and leaned over the rag-wiped rail
of the bar. His hair was wet with grease, and his shirt was freckled
white from scratching his scalp. In high school, when we would skip
class and smoke cigarettes in the breezeway, he would always say,

*We're from the North End. You gotta act like you're not from here
if you want to ever get out.* I could barely understand him, until now,
at *Newtz*, drunk and not acknowledging those wasted years between us.
Sam was at the other end of the bar, drinking until he was slurring
at two bikers in the far corner with their motorcycle club patches.

He started pointing and calling them names, and I knew to look away.
I took myself outside, but the men dragged Sam outside, seconds later,
by his neck and arms. They slapped a bottle across his jaw,
and his body crumpled like a crushed can. The men kicked him,
and I watched his head roll back and forth. I hid in the dark, wishing

for easier ways to forget where we were from. When the men were done
they leaned over Sam's body with a cellphone and took a picture.

A flash filled the beaten quiet. When the doorway to the bar was hollow
with light, I stood over Sam. I wanted to make sure he was breathing.
His throat sounded like a muffler about to rust off. Even though

he was knocked out, his eyes were open, and he stared up at the sky.
The sky held a few stars like a cupped hand full of teeth. He couldn't see
any of it, and I turned to go back inside, jealous of how he'd come to—
the gravel under his shoes sounding like his joints as he rose—jealous
of how he'd wince at the blood on his shirt and not know where he was.

NORTH END IV

At the Illinois State Fair, in Happy Hollow,
passed the Tilt-a-Whirl's grinding orbit and the nauseating rise of Pharaoh's Swing,
a man impersonating Abraham Lincoln
delivers his House Divided speech

to a group of cowlicked boys and girls who listen
less to his words and more to the crunching of corn dogs and elephant ears
inside their mouths as they marvel at Honest Abe balancing on stilts.

Of everything important—a spectacle of distraction has been made.

In the Coors Light tent, the parents drop
plastic beer cups into piles of plastic beer cups. Last hour and last call
at the fair, and I'm stopped by a politician under a tent, running for Governor.

Springfield is a word inside his mouth. He wants to leave this place,
head back north to Chicago—which is not the capital—
when all of this is over. Too many people just like him have shaken my hand
only to call anything south of the city *a shitty place to live.*

He makes me think that I have more in common with the stuffed prize animals
being crammed back into their shipping boxes
or the smaller rides being dismantled and stacked into truck beds.

A quarter of the lightbulbs on the fair's exit arch
are out, and through the numbered streets and slab-lot houses clustered together,
cordoned off by half-rotten picket fences
with yards full of truck cabs and car parts,

an ornamental crystal ball calls to me
like some last ditch effort in faith,
but I can't tell the future from the present
no matter how long I stare into its shape.

LAST RITES

Before he got sick and was laid off, Lee always let me leave early
from our parking garage without clocking out, so I felt like I owed him
when he called and asked me to visit. As soon as I arrived

I had to use the bathroom. Drops of his blood dotted the toilet rim,
and his teeth were floating in a glass of water. When I saw them,
it felt like stumbling upon someone I knew naked—turning

to hide from each other after we had already locked eyes for a second.
I didn't know I'd be bearing witness to Lee's private dismantling,
the quiet, brutal ways the body forces open its doors.

On the couch, he asked me to sit. He shifted his weight into me.
The air smelled like old furniture and crotch rot. The sharpness
of his skinny legs pushed against mine, and I said *yes* when he asked

if I wanted to see pictures from Europe, from his forties and fifties.
My real life is there, he said. He wanted to go back but he was hooked
to Springfield by a catheter bag and plastic sheets on the couch

sticking to his skin. The next pictures were of a boy
even younger than me—fifteen or sixteen. The boy's head rested
on Lee's shoulder while Lee laid a hand on his thigh. The boy

had a forced smile, bruises on his neck, and a blanket covering his lap.
These pictures were an admittance into the unshared parts of his life.
After that, Lee asked me if I would help him to his bedroom.

The house nurse was gone so I looped his arm in mine and guided him
to the adjustable bed. I pulled the covers over him. *Thank you.*
It's just been so long, he said, extending his arms like a small boy reaching

for a thing that has been taken from him and placed on a high shelf.
I leaned over him and hugged him goodbye. When he pressed his mouth
to mine, I let him. I let the coarse hair of his upper lip scrape my cheek

as I pulled away. It sounded like the dead leaves scratching through
our parking garage when it was empty, when the concrete echoed
with unforgivable disregard for the last attendant on shift at night.

Lee reached for me when I turned to leave, but I couldn't help him die
like that. I didn't have that kind of mercy. Now, I think maybe I was
a coward, and I wonder about all the other choices I could have made.

SELF-PORTRAIT AS PSYCHIATRIC WARD

My doors auto-lock. I am a room where the windows don't open and bodies line up single file and swallow underwater feelings. I am an aquarium. I am a toilet bowl full of goldfish forgetting their lives one day at a time. At night, I hold your sleeping fires close, your dreams of crows and dried butterflies pinned to felt. I collect those in a web of needles. My deck of cards is so creased and faded no one knows what hearts to play. My stampede surges gently in the swing of capricious days and capsules stuffed with more days. Crosses and crucifixes on every wall make the loudest sounds. Calendars checked with craft days to play with clay and mold the face of Christ. Or a shoe. I am your nails bitten and chewed because I don't let you cut, so you cut. Everything in me is sharp until you leave. When I open my mouth, I speak in purple hyacinth petals that fill the ward with wilting and dead leaves and belt buckles. I am a cold tremor, a shiver, a skull cracking on linoleum. I am a system of wires, a buckling of knees, pale bodies arching from bedframes until I can push them out—some calmer fear—back into the world where gardens are bright and lush colored, where birds fly in unpredictable patterns and there is an emergency every day.

DEFINITIONS OF *BODY*

Body 1. "Of Work": My mother did not—collected disability in the mail. The body is a paycheck inside an envelope held up to the light. 2. "Of Water": My mother was a river, carried me into a gulf. When I was thirteen I searched through the trash can to find the sunken orange bottles that resurfaced among eggshells and coffee grounds. She pulled herself under her own current. 3. "Of Bones": Her skull was a bag of voices. When she breathed, her rib cage moved like fingertips tapping together. Her teeth turned yellow, then white, then ghosts. She swallowed her ghosts, until she filled up with too many. 4. "Of Christ": Has risen. Revived at the hospital. The blood put back into her body with blood. The way I stood in the dark room and touched the IV hole to make sure she was real. 5. "Of Lies": Erased. She is not real. Her intention is to be a wraith. When she wakes and I ask how she is, my mother looks past me. 6. "Of Proof": The note I found that read, *I'm just so tired. I love you all tender. Goodnight.*

OUR MOTHER STOLEN IN A POTHOLE

I'm not kidding when I say the boy's last name was Sabbath,
and he knew everything I needed; *Life's short, let's make it shorter*,
he'd say. We both had a sense of a loss falling through us
like a hammer brought to an anvil. Those sparks struck

from our bodies—we went into the night to reclaim them.
When Sabbath dared me to steal a statue of the Virgin Mary
from someone's yard, I did. Back on his front porch,
Sabbath drew a 666 and a satanic star across Mary's blue veil

with a black sharpie. If there was time for a miracle, this was it—
a vexed statue crying blood would not have shocked me.
I'd been waiting for an identical replica of Mary to cry blood
for my mother as she looked down from the dresser, surrounded

by orange bottles like offertory candles. My mother would pray all day
to Mary from underneath weighted blankets, and I'd watch
from a crack in her door, watch her pray forever without recovering.
I'm still waiting. Sabbath was gripping that sharpie over crying Mary

when I asked him to stop, told him it wasn't funny anymore. So he rose,
walked into South Grand Avenue and set her inside the hollow
of a pothole. *It'd be a miracle if she were saved before a car comes and hits her*,
Sabbath said, and I thought again of my mother, how she wanted

to be like Mary and leave the planet, ascend into the schizophrenic
version of heaven locking its wrought iron gates inside her brain.
Inside Sabbath's house, while the television covered us in its light,
I clamped clothespins onto my fingers out of boredom, tapping

and scaling my fingers across the floor humming *Bloody Sunday*.
I was looking for synchronicity in that moment, and I found it
humming for the Virgin in the pothole, stretching her arms out
to an oncoming car, welcoming the barreling steel into her

like a sickness she never asked for, smashing her stone body
off the planet into pieces, into a vision of heaven I'll never know,
while my fingers became piano keys and the sad music I made
couldn't put her body back together or follow where she went.

NORTH END V

After dawn the air is the color of a clean spoon, on Factory and Ridge,
past Lincoln Yellow Cab,
                                        where I walk to work
and old memories retrieve themselves

        before broken concrete replaces them
                                        with the bar boarded up, tap-dry and empty,
abandoned. That bar stares forever across the dividing train tracks

at a parking lot full of rust-blue school buses
        once filled with the deafening sounds of childhood
                unconcerned and unmoved by memory.

In those same weed-thick and gravel-loose ditches
        men gather this morning by the tracks trying to squeeze out
the last words the night has left wet and slurred across their tongues.

                        They have stayed up so long
nothing seems like it will end.
                Their last words mean everything to them.

They should take a cab home but they will stumble,
        or more unfortunately lay down drunk
and baffled in that same ditch where my friends and I would

guddle for each other like awkward fish in a slow and shallow river bend,

where our fists would send one another home
all red in the face, out of breath, forcing each other to be proud
        of where we were from.

BAPTISM

For the three years I was your boyfriend, your mother had me mow the lawn.
  I'd ride my bike over, pulling my mower behind me along uneven roads
because your father left in his truck years ago with his mower and other parts
  of your life unreadable as fog. A rusted rake leaned against the house
in place of him. A hornet's nest hid in the eave of the rotting stoop awning,
  its frame like gauze wrap was guarded by drones. They heard me cutting
too close and swarmed. I released the handle brake to stings and burning,
  and I ran inside. You were washing yourself in a mold-spotted shower
You're fine. Help empty the tub and calm down, you said. Under the showerhead,
  you shivered like someone stuck outside in the cold under a dying trickle
of colder rain. I bailed the standing water out with a bucket and pretended
  I could stop your house from sinking. Bath water filled the pink toilet.
Paw-spilled cat litter caked my knees. Something always needed changed—
  the sink lights dotted with fruit flies, the broken shower drain, the shit-
filled litter box in the corner. One cat nudged the door open with her head.
  You looked down at me, wrung the rag and laid it limp across the back
of my raw neck. I handed you a towel and you guided me to your bedroom.
  In here, you said. Your mother was at work. The window unit sputtered
like an idling lawn mower. I didn't say anything. *Sit down and relax*, you said.
  We were too young to be alone. Here were our bodies anyway.

DAGUERREOTYPE

swirling toward me as I dine outside

the clamor and chorus of silverware

makes my teeth hunger and hurt

from cotillion snapshots taken at prom

you look like porcelain in ornate taffeta

my hands pluck a seed from each sequin

loss grows exhausted from this loam

across a fake Italian landscape

our lifetimes now separated by lifetimes

at a Springfield café spilling water alone

your memory is a thin cloud of gnats

folded and pressed into white-lace napkins

I am reminded of a future we tried to make

skeletal bobby pins in your bouffant

milk stitches weave your body close

unraveling you apart like years

like skin around an old ankle bone

a styrofoam trellis a blue camera spark

guilt flattening laughter into a line

over your face so young and always here

CONFIRMATION

You taught me how hands could be laid, how they could touch
    a head and heal, but all of those hands eventually fell limp
like a field bent by threshing or a lit match dropped in water. Once,
    we used to dance in The Corner Tavern's neon light
where the pickup exhaust wafted inside like harvest dust.
    Life in the Midwest is like one long goodbye because life is the same
everyday, and I didn't realize you had left until there was nothing
    but hard work and long days ending with the wind's silent dirge
that sounds like trying not to die but always dies in smaller ways—
    screen doors that slam shut but don't shut all the way
because the house has settled and the roof is warping from the sky
    boiling over with thunder and rain. I wake up now to the flashing
falling from the gutters and the water dripping through the holes
    in the ceiling. All I do is recall your voice like a prayer thrashing
my skull that mines the night begging our fathers our fathers
    our fathers in prayer, but they are off begging other women
in other towns. This town is not the memory I want, but I know
    how sadness works. It's like a kettle-bottom collapsing onto
the details of every thought. I shouldn't have, but I stayed in town
    to try and keep what I love alive, but no that never works. We were
a long time ago and a long time ago is too hard to get back.
    The last time we talked you said, *We will end up like our mothers*—
waiting for nothing. Then you didn't come back. No. Not ever.

NORTH END VI

        Almost every holy Sunday after Church I would get shot
by twin boys with broken Nerf guns
                when my father would take me to Jungle Jim's Café
on Peoria, between the Harley bar and the dilapidated house,
       where the twins must have lived a long time
shooting customers and pretending to protect their territory.

           Inside the diner, the adolescent slogans of excuse:
Guns don't kill people, people kill people,
              and I almost talked like that,
but it never sounded right. It sounded like someone not thinking hard enough.

       I had no choice but to stare at the pictures of Nascar drivers
adorned in Christmas lights, the singing parrot, and the pleading Barbie
          the owner Jim had hung up on a makeshift zip line
of string and coat hangers.

           The atmosphere of grease, flat soda, and the vague smell
of oil changes was at one time a kind of heaven someone tried to teach me,
       but the torn vinyl seating and the smoke curling upwards
             didn't look like any paradise.

Sometimes I heard mention of Hell's Angels, but I never saw any angels back then.
     I never saw any wings,
             except the door to the kitchen
that flapped and flapped. Maybe it was a guardian angel
      that got tired of his job
and slumped over Jim's counter and asked where I was from.
         I answered, *A lifelong Northender,* just like my father would say.
Yeah, life's real long till it ain't, the guardian angel said, laughing
           like someone who had just lit a fire.

We walked back to the car after eating
and heard weed whackers laboring in the distance,

                     not unlike how blood cycles through our veins—
but that laughter, I'm glad it's far away,

                       so faint now I can hardly hear it.

WHAT I MEAN WHEN I SAY *I DON'T BOX ANYMORE*

I'm thinking of that summer we played Russian roulette
with the six-shot revolver Seth stole from his grandfather's closet.

The two of us each taking one turn, spinning and pulling. Each of us
exhaling after the click. Neither of us wanted to die, but we were young

and needed someone to die, so we could feel guilty and learn how it feels
to carry that guilt. We pressed the barrel between our teeth and bit the steel.

We quoted our favorite lines wrong on purpose before pulling the trigger—
Everything's beautiful. Everything hurts. It was like spinning a globe

and quickly pressing your finger down somewhere on land or over water
and if your finger hits water you spin again—but we didn't spin again

because our mothers were asleep at home in small beds dreaming of us
or not dreaming of us, and what if the hammer had punched the bullet—

then nothing? We were left with the guilt of being lucky. Somewhere
a clock went on spinning and pulling itself into a new day that kept turning

brighter and begging of me something I had to admit—that risking
my body would not stop the world from ruining my body, or stop

my mother from forgetting to live. When I came home smelling of sweat
and alcohol, I walked into my mother's room. The drugs had her sleeping.

I said something like, *I know why you want to die,* and I kissed her on the forehead
while she went on sleeping, dreaming of me or not dreaming of me.

I walked to the garage to practice the hitting I knew how to do
and the hitting I knew how to take. Under the hum of a 40-watt bulb,

I imbedded the cracks of a heavy bag's dry leather with my sweaty hands.
This time I didn't wrap my fists with tape or gloves, and after twenty minutes

of punching myself out, my knuckles split open, blood began to smear,
the chain squeaked, and the bag spun around on its anchored hook.

A BRIEF HISTORY OF FRIENDS

Seth and Chris were brothers, and I lived with them that summer
I didn't know I was living. They were like me. They smelled like corn
and had small fingernails. Seth would force Chris and I to fight
inside the dog kennel, and Chris would bust my nose open then press
against me the way some boys press themselves against other boys.

Afterward, Seth would hose us off with cold water, but the fights stopped
that summer when empty spaces began forming inside their grandfather's skull.
He almost set fire to his house with an unfinished thought. He started
to forget our names, and he even forgot the name of his only friend
George, who started dating Seth and Chris' mother that summer, too.

George explained to us how their grandfather was slipping in and out of time,
when their grandfather kept asking, *Who are all of you?* George stuck around
and refused to let strangers take care of his friend. That's why George drove us
to their grandfather's house every day. He wrapped our faces with t-shirts,
and we scrubbed their grandfather's shit from the carpet. George bought us food,

and it felt nice to have a job. Weeks later, Seth and Chris's grandfather
was taken away in an ambulance. George was pale in the face when he explained
to Seth and Chris' mother that he wasn't going to see his friend go out
like that, and later that night, a nurse found George holding a plastic bag
over the face of his friend inside the ER. George ran out of the hospital,

but a police alert ran in the paper the next day, and the next day George
sat at the kitchen table pleading, *I'm sorry I'm sorry*, to their mother
while she said, *Don't you goddamn bother*. George stammered on about *Christ*
and *Love* until the next day we found George in the basement, hanging
from a support beam. Before he kicked the stool over, I imagine his face settled

like a small house in the middle of a field beaten by wind, and as he fell,
the wide open screen door was thrown shut—a snap—as George's body swung
back and forth in the dark all night missing his friend. The next day, nothing

was over, and their mother cried, *No No No,* like an engine that refuses to start.
Chris was on the porch and his eyes looked like the car windows we shot out

with BB guns, and I had the urge to touch him softly, too. He watched Seth
and I haul from the house the used things of a finished life. When George's case
of small minted coins fell to the curb, I didn't ask if I could take them.
I slipped them into my pocket. Seth and I locked eyes and for a long time
he looked as if he wanted to hit me, but he shrugged. It felt real. It felt good.

ON FIGHTING

Honest to God—it felt like someone dropped lit matches
inside my skull, turned my head into a tinderbox, a raw thing.

I had been hurt the way a child can only be hurt by his mother,

and those motherless days were made of boys that turned my brain
into blue sparks when they'd connect their fists to my chin.

From a distance we might have appeared as startling as a knife

abruptly flipped open. Most of the time, on uneven ground,
we'd throw hooks and haymakers then backpedal scared.

I never got knocked out. No—not once.

But honest to God, my vision got so small and narrow sometimes
I thought I was going to shut off. Afterward, we'd help each other up,

dust each other off, my friends and I, and talk about what it felt like

to shake someone's hand after they had spent a great deal of time
trying to hurt us. I have a lot of different names

for what to call that feeling. Sometimes *mercy*. Sometimes *all of this*

is necessary. Sometimes *one day we will all be loved but not yet*. Truth is,
I was never that skilled at slipping punches or finding angles

or pivoting out of the way. I just didn't want to be alone.

It was fun to stand there flat-footed
and let God answer in that hard way he likes to touch a body.

LOVE IS LIKE A HORSE SET ON FIRE FROM THE INSIDE

The smell of fresh cut grass is in the air.
Which means the rain has let up. Which means today I'm going to try
                        and drive forever again. Which means to leave
and hunt for a feeling I haven't thought about in a long time.
        A feeling goes extinct when it becomes a thought,
and I'm thinking

how I tried to tell someone who knew more than me that I loved him.

                    Which means I will never be able to do the right thing
because love is like a horse set on fire from the inside—

        just look what happened to that old city
        when all those men came pouring out

like feelings they never bothered to tame. That's why I'm trying to leave
        again Which means I have ruined most things in my life.
Which means from now on I have to live in a constant state of movement
                    and absence. Which means anger will never find me
again. Hopefully. Every hundred miles

        a Cracker Barrel, an adult video store, something
claiming to be the world's largest, and all of that must be important
                        to someone,
but every hundred miles, I'm reminded of home. Which means I'm thinking

about the length of Illinois.
            Another hundred miles and my feet are knife-numb
from sitting so when I take an exit ramp off I-57 and get gas,

            I stand there and wait for my body to come back.
        I wait for feeling to return. Which means my tongue
    is a language preserved in a cave of ice, extinct for a time
and waiting for the thaw. Which means I'm waiting

for a reason to speak again, a reason to say *if this isn't good enough*
    then I don't know what is—the slight breeze while the pump
        fills the tank. Which means maybe it is possible to come home
            from nowhere. Which means I, too, can be a good person.

Which means there are many different kinds of beauty.

WILD VISION OF WHAT IS REAL

I had to piss in water bottles when I worked the parking booth
at the city wrestling meet since no one came by to give me a break,
so I was already uncomfortable when a mother appeared needing me

to call the police. *This lady just started cursing at me and my son. She spit at us.*
She threatened me, the mother said. This other woman was in the walkway.
On her wrist was a white bracelet that she was running through her hair,

thin and unwashed. She was yelling about being raped and beaten
and left to the devil by this mother who had appeared in front of me.
I didn't know what to do or how to help anyone except to explain

the situation to the 911 operator while the woman continued to threaten
the mother. The son had the look of a boy realizing for the first time
his mother had a body that could be damaged—that his own mother

could be stolen into danger, into its wild vision of what is real.
I don't know why but the woman snapped—Y*our ass is getting beat.*
That's it. The mother took three steps back, stuck out her arms,

while the woman charged her. I stepped out of the booth and grabbed
the other woman, saying, *Please stop now. It's okay. Please.*
I don't remember if I meant it, or if I was just trying to stop someone

from getting hit. I don't know how to talk about her body,
but it was twitching, and I could feel the spit lisping from her lips
onto my neck. I wanted to apologize for grabbing her. I asked her

if she was okay, and I tried to look her in the eyes, but she didn't even know
I was holding her. It only took a few minutes for the police to arrive,
take her by the arms and explain they got a lot of calls about this woman,

especially in this area of town. There was nothing to do but drive her back
to her group home. She let the police guide her to the back of their car
and she was gone. Maybe if I hadn't been at work I would have gone, too.

I would have waited with her in the back of the car and waited again
inside the sterile bedroom of her group home that smelled like antiseptic
and bleach, and I would have waited until she was done thrashing

with the terror that tore and tore at her body because nothing was her fault.
I would have, but I was at work. The mother thanked me for calling the police
on that *crazy woman* while her son took off toward the convention center.

She said she had another son wrestling in a few minutes, and she hoped
they wouldn't be late. I nodded, but I hoped they were late. I hoped
her son got pinned down by his arms while the crowd cheered,

while I stood in the middle of a parking lot wishing that woman
would have heard me say, *I'm sorry.* I wished there was a way to let her
know that I knew she wasn't crazy, but she was gone and there was a car

pulling up to the sliding door of my booth with a *Lanphier High Wrestling*
bumper sticker. The man driving was looking around, trying to figure out
who to pay, which way to turn, because he wanted to go, too.

SOMETIMES I CALL THE DAMAGE HEALING

when I'm walking home alone, which means everyone is gone
and done with me. Healing is just one name for it—

all the hands that have praised me

and baptized my body with rocks, when their hands made me
slop home with blood across crushed lips like a mouthful of blackberry juice.

I mean it when I said I'm a goddamn lickspittle

to the setting sun, grinning its last wide smile on the horizon
like a slice of apple. In the evening and on my way to grace

my cheekbone with a bag of snowpeas,

I pause at the muddy bank of the millpond and watch herons

pitch and rush the late light while the dragonflies nibble the crappie
bubbles that flinch the water's surface like a window holding captive

some last breath. Uselessness

is another name I have for it—all the hands clenched in prayer,
praying for me to defend the side of town where I was from

or some other insignificant part of my life

that the boys of the Midwest have deemed worthy of confession.
But most of the time I name the damage healing when I slingshot stones

at the crickets sweeping their legs

against the cordgrass and pickerelweed, when the waterwheel races
the water down from the trough, and it sounds like peace at last—

a trickle of water, the quiet throbbing inside the body after pain.

AND OTHER ACTS OF MERCY

When has it not been raining? When will the smoothed furrow of gravel and silt
be given calm so that it can fondly recall the flooded creek that quenched its thirst?
On one of those frequent nights when I couldn't see clearly when the rain was looking
down into the ringing basin of my life and the odd sounds it has made,

I noticed a thing moving in the middle of the road. Only after the car
cut up the trees with its headlights, begetting the feeling something great
was following me or someone was leaving me for good, was the turtle spared.
Cloud-soaked and chilled, I lifted the turtle up to the trees

twisting their arthritic fingers of moss and bark. I'm sure there were faces
in those trees, too, storm-molded faces and faces begging for eyes and ears
so they could see and hear as I raised the turtle above my head to speak
to him as he withdrew into his shell and how many times have I shown thanks

by hiding and withdrawing into a hard and freakish shape? I laid the turtle down
on the embankment and watched him slide down into the ditch's safety
where the collecting water would wash the road from his belly and where, like me,
however slow, he could begin again looking for something so perfect it never ends.

UPON LEARNING THAT YEARS LATER THE WORLD DID NOT END, I WAS FINALLY ABLE TO TALK ABOUT THE WILD HORSES

After John Murillo

A white screen door opened then slammed shut dragging the idleness
of streetlights and dogs barking in the distance from their straw-thin beds

as a boy wiped his mouth on a paper towel dotting it red. It was 1999,
and after the boy dragged the long nights of that year in behind him

the Chicago Cubs were on TV about to lose in the thirteenth inning.
Not much happened that year but panic. Early August and the humidity

was as heavy as any hand across any jaw. My father's hand. My jaw.
I'm the boy in this poem. I was only ten and wanting to smoke a cigarette

before the world ended. When my father caught me, I tasted blood.
The end of the world was going to taste like blood. And when I ran inside,

a Y2K commercial flashed the screen with its upsetting reminder.
I was only ten but starting to realize I loved everyone, and didn't

want anyone to die that year, but the commercial implied there would be
mobs in the street made up of all the people we loved. In Springfield,

in our backyard, I sat on cinder blocks watching my father burn
leaf barrels as he spoke of these mobs and the people they would kill.

Did you know that a feral group of horses was once called a mob, too?
I had a mobile of horses when I was little that ran in circles and made music

above my crib. I guess everything we love turns violent—even a group of horses
and the people we trust. But I'm alive in another life now, retelling

a version of it from a place of eminence, a softer world, where fear
and panic are reimagined as fog-dewed pastures reaching for the last pink

cloud of evening. And in 1999, when I say I stood there with a smear of blood
on my face watching the Y2K commercial leave the screen like blue smoke

lifting to a Budweiser commercial featuring Dalmatians and Clydesdales,
I mean I saw how everything was connected—My father's hand. My jaw.

1999 and I wanted those Clydesdales to break free, become a mob and run away
as violent as my father's hand. I wanted them to turn into the mobs

that would break the windows at the end of the world. 1999 and I knew
there was a baby somewhere with his own mobile of piebald horses

making music, and that's all he would know of the world before it ended.
And all I know would be the taste of blood and smoke and music. 1999

and days later, a mob of kids cornered me on the playground and palmed
my face against the wrench-bent coils of a chain-link fence. My khakis

knee-torn when they threw me down across the asphalt and demanded back
a collection of baseball cards I never stole. Their hands. My jaw.

1999 and years later when that life was over, I drove to Eminence, Missouri
and stood on a root-raised hill watching a mob of wild horses run

as peaceful as a world that never ended. Eminence, Missouri—
the only place in the Midwest that still contains a mob of wild horses.

They are what's left to say about the wind. Their hooves mow down
the muzzle-high wheatgrass and my father's hand is a thing I shake now.

My jaw, a healed bone calm enough to speak of violence, to contain its taste,
to drop in awe when the mob leaves, lifting away like fists from years ago.

GUIDE AND GUARD US FAR AND NEAR

I was a lost boy with a quiet ache, so quiet it was like an egg yolk breaking
inside my mouth. I could only feel the taste. I couldn't see the color

like the sun setting while my back was turned. Each night I've ever lived
and reflected upon is a painting I have stared too long at, unable to articulate

or differentiate between the strokes and contrasts. This landscape—
catalogued by my past into a museum of ache—gets harrow-scraped

and exhales harvest dust while the cornfields shed their gold.
So many layers to it all and I've grown content out here in the chill,

watching the tractors cut beans late into the night. Enough dark liquor
and those lost songs I used to sing at church with my mother come back.

Enough dark liquor and the voices of everything I have forgotten
start to fall backward from memory. What else is there to do but rest

my boots on this crooked porch and try to sing—*Lady, help the absent loved ones.*
How we miss their presence here. May the hand of thy protection guide and guard them

far and near. I still don't know how the rest of it goes, but I'm going to stay up
all night. Enough dark liquor and I no longer miss what I have lost. I was a lost boy

with a quiet ache, so quiet it was like waiting, and I've waited so long
for one more good sleep—the kind that comes after there are no other choices

to be made, and the mind's worries shrink to gnat-sized ripples in a pond.
Tomorrow is another night so, maybe, bless me, Lord, with one more sunset

where the sky turns to the feeling of sweat drying. Let me slip into that state of luck
where the trees release their tight grip and relax like out-of-tune guitar strings

that still have a lot of life left, where their bristling sounds like a voice
making its way through radio static. Oh, I think the trees are breathing

please against my cold skin. *Please* is all I hear now *Please, Please, Please*—
and that is all the permission I need to make it through another night leaving.

NOTES

The lines "Lady, help the absent loved ones. How we miss their presence here. May the hand of Thy protection Guide and guard them far and near" included in the poems "Hymn" and "Guide Us Far and Near" are taken from the Catholic hymn "Mother Dearest, Mother Fairest." Original author and composer are unknown.

The Pillsbury Plant referenced in "Vandalism" is on Fifteenth Street and Phillips in Springfield, Illinois. It opened in 1929. It was sold in 1999 and closed for good in 2001. It was purchased for salvage in 2008. There is currently a cleanup effort underway.

The bar referenced in "Thin Napkins Sprinkled with Salt" is now closed and has since been renamed.

On March 12, 2006, a tornado hit Springfield, Illinois, and took the head off of the "Lauterbach Tire Muffler Man" or "Lauterbach Giant." The head was reattached three days later. Photos of the statue were originally published in the *State-Journal Register*.

In "On Fighting," the line "I had been hurt the way a child can only be hurt by his mother" is paraphrased from the short story "Dirty Wedding" by Denis Johnson.

The poem "Upon Learning That Years Later the World Did Not End, I Was Finally Able To Talk about the Wild Horses" is formally inspired by John Murillo's poem "Upon Reading That Eric Dolphy Transcribed Even the Calls of Certain Species of Birds."

ACKNOWLEDGMENTS

Thank you to the editors of the following journals in which these poems first appeared, sometimes in earlier forms:

American Literary Review: "Noise Falling Backward" (as: "Noise Falling Backwards")
Best New Poets 2015: "Definitions of *Body*"
Columbia Poetry Review: "Pie Tins behind Porch Lights" and "Word Problem"
Copper Nickel: "North End III"
december: "What I Mean When I Say *I Don't Box Anymore*"
Fifth Wednesday: "North End I"
Jabberwock Review: "Self-Portrait as Stolen Bike"
Hayden's Ferry Review: "Flyover Country"
Hobart: "Self-Portrait as Home Run Ball"
Midwestern Gothic: "The Decapitation of Paul Bunyan"
New Ohio Review: "Confirmation"
New South: "Self-Portrait as Psychiatric Ward"
Passages North: "Switchgrass"
The Pinch: "Hymn"
Redivider: "Daguerreotype"
TriQuarterly: "Scared Violent Like Horses" and "As If the Shirt Were Standing Up Straight, Hand Raised"
Sycamore Review: "Cremation"
ZiN Daily: "On Fighting"
Zone 3: "Baptism" and "Sometimes I Call the Damage Healing"

* * *

Thank you to Tracy K. Smith for selecting "Definitions of Body" for inclusion in *Best New Poets 2015*. Thank you to Alex Lemon for selecting "Hymn" as the 2016 winner of *The Pinch* Literary Award in Poetry. Thank you to Hannah Stephenson and the late Okla Elliott for including "Definitions of Body" in the *New Poetry from the Midwest 2017* anthology published by New American Press.

Thank you to Allison Joseph, Judy Jordan, Jon Tribble, and Jennifer Franny Key for your mentorship and instruction. I am eternally grateful to the time spent and life I was allowed to live in southern Illinois. Thank you to everyone in the Southern Illinois University Carbondale Creative Writing Program.

Thank you to Andrew Hemmert, Meghann Plunkett, Anna Knowles, and Jacqui Zeng for your friendship, close readings, late-night advice, as well as climbing to the edge of the cliff with me.

Thank you to Jessica Suchon, Josh Myers, Kirk Schlueter, Teresa Dzieglewicz, James Dunlap, Meg Flannery, and Mary Kate Varnau for your friendship, support, and trivia skills.

Thank you to Joanna Beth Tweedy, David Logan, Judi O'Brien Anderson, Jim Warner, Amy Sayre-Baptista, Lisa Higgs, and Tracy Zeman for being the original guiding light and encouraging me to take up the life I am living now.

Thank you to Sara Eliza Johnson and Matt Rasmussen for your thoughtful reads and kind words.

Thank you to Alda Sigurðardóttir and Kristveig Halldórsdóttir for allowing me time to write some of these poems at the Gullkistan Center for Creative People in Laugarvatn, Iceland, and for the community that they foster and support. Thank you to Natalija Grgorinić and Ognjen Rađen for the time at the Zvona i Nari Library and Literary Retreat in Ližnjan, Croatia, which allowed me time and space to revise some of these poems and to explore parts of this world close to my heart.

Thank you to the wonderful editorial and design teams at Milkweed Editions for your positive energy and support in helping put this book into the world.

Thank you to Wayne Miller and the team at *Copper Nickel* for honoring the work of Jake Adam York and for making this prize possible.

Thank you to Victoria Chang—and I can't thank you enough—for selecting this manuscript and for sharing in the complex beauty, vulnerability, and sensitivity that is life.

Thank you to my Mother and Father. I love you. Thank you to my family and friends back in the 217. I carry all of you with me.

Thank you to Rachel Jamison Webster and Adele for your love, optimism, and joy.

And thank *you* for reading this book and holding it in your hands.

JOHN MCCARTHY is the author of one previous collection, *Ghost County*, which was named a Best Poetry Book of 2016 by the *Chicago Review of Books*. McCarthy is the 2016 winner of *The Pinch* Literary Award in Poetry, and his work has appeared in *Best New Poets 2015*, *Haydon's Ferry Review*, *Passages North*, *Sycamore Review*, *Zone 3*, and in anthologies such as *New Poetry from the Midwest 2017*. He received his MFA in creative writing from Southern Illinois University Carbondale and serves as an editor of *RHINO* magazine and *Quiddity* International Literary Journal and Public-Radio Program. He lives in Illinois.

The Jake Adam York Prize for a first or second collection of poems was established in 2016 to honor the name and legacy of Jake Adam York (1972–2012). York was the founder of *Copper Nickel*, a nationally distributed literary journal at the University of Colorado Denver. His work as a poet and scholar explored memory and social history, and particularly the Civil Rights Movement.

The judge for the 2017 Jake Adam York Prize was Victoria Chang.

milkweed
editions

Founded as a nonprofit organization in 1980, Milkweed Editions is an independent publisher. Our mission is to identify, nurture and publish transformative literature, and build an engaged community around it.

milkweed.org